BEGINNERS GUIDE ON HOW TO START A COFFEE TRUCK

A Successful and Easy Step to Start, Open and Run a Profit Oriented Business

Gabriel Taylor

TABLE OF CONTENTS

Chapter 1

Introduction to the Coffee Truck Business

The mobile coffee business has become a thriving industry, offering entrepreneurs a unique and flexible way to bring the coffee experience directly to customers. In this chapter, we will delve into the essential aspects of starting a coffee truck business, providing a comprehensive introduction to this dynamic and rewarding venture.

Overview of the Mobile Coffee Industry

The mobile coffee industry has experienced a remarkable surge in popularity, driven by a societal shift towards convenience and a growing appreciation for high-quality coffee experiences outside traditional cafes. This section provides an in-depth exploration of the current state of the mobile coffee industry, shedding light on the factors that have propelled its exponential growth.

Exponential Growth and Demand:

The mobile coffee industry's meteoric rise can be attributed to the increasing demand for convenient and premium coffee on the go. Modern lifestyles, characterized by a fast-paced rhythm, have created a need for accessible and quick solutions to caffeine cravings. Mobile coffee trucks perfectly align with this demand, offering a solution that transcends the constraints of traditional brick-and-mortar cafes. The ease of access and the ability to cater to diverse locations, from busy streets to remote outdoor events, have fueled the industry's popularity among consumers seeking a satisfying cup of coffee wherever they are.

Versatility in Locations:

Mobile coffee trucks have successfully diversified their presence, making them a ubiquitous sight in a variety of settings. Whether it's catering to morning commuters in bustling urban areas, providing a caffeine fix at outdoor festivals, or becoming a welcome addition to corporate gatherings, these mobile enterprises have demonstrated unparalleled adaptability. The ability to reach consumers in different locations not only broadens the customer base but also enhances the overall experience of enjoying a cup of coffee.

Unique and Personalized Experiences:

One of the driving forces behind the success of the mobile coffee industry is its ability to provide a unique and personalized experience for coffee enthusiasts. Unlike traditional coffee shops, mobile coffee trucks offer a sense of novelty and immediacy. Customers can witness the preparation of their beverages on the spot, engaging in a more intimate and interactive coffee-drinking experience. This personalized touch creates a memorable connection between the consumer and the brand, fostering loyalty and repeat business.

Key Trends and Market Dynamics:

Understanding the current trends and market dynamics is crucial for navigating the competitive landscape of the mobile coffee industry. This explores the emergence of specialty coffee blends, the increasing focus on sustainable practices, and the integration of technology for mobile ordering and payment. By staying attuned to these trends, entrepreneurs can position their coffee trucks strategically to meet evolving consumer preferences and stay ahead of the curve.

Factors Contributing to Success:

The success of the mobile coffee industry is underpinned by various factors, including a commitment to quality, innovative marketing strategies, and the ability to create a memorable brand identity. This section will delve into these critical success factors, offering insights into how aspiring entrepreneurs can leverage them to establish and sustain a thriving mobile coffee business.

The overview of the mobile coffee industry presented in this section highlights the industry's remarkable growth, the versatility of mobile coffee trucks, the emphasis on unique and personalized experiences, key market trends, and the factors that contribute to success. Armed with this knowledge, entrepreneurs can embark on their journey into the mobile coffee business with a solid understanding of the industry landscape and the dynamics that drive its ongoing success.

Market Analysis and Trends

Embarking on a successful coffee truck business requires a comprehensive understanding of the market landscape. This section emphasizes the critical importance of conducting a thorough market analysis before diving into the business. Through the identification of competitors, understanding customer preferences, and recognizing emerging trends, entrepreneurs can make informed decisions that lay the foundation for a thriving coffee truck enterprise.

Identifying Potential Competitors:

The first step in market analysis involves a meticulous examination of existing and potential competitors. Understanding the local coffee landscape is crucial for determining market saturation, identifying gaps in services, and pinpointing areas where a mobile coffee business can thrive. Entrepreneurs need to assess not only other coffee trucks but also traditional cafes, kiosks, and other beverage providers in the chosen location. Analyzing competitors provides valuable insights into their strengths, weaknesses, and unique selling propositions, allowing entrepreneurs to position their coffee truck strategically.

Understanding Customer Preferences:

Successful market analysis hinges on a deep understanding of customer preferences. This involves not only identifying the demographics of the target audience but also delving into their specific tastes, habits, and expectations regarding coffee consumption. Surveys, focus groups, and observational research can be employed to gather valuable data on what customers look for in their coffee experience. By aligning menu offerings and services with these preferences, entrepreneurs can tailor their coffee truck to meet the unique demands of their target market, creating a more compelling value proposition.

Recognizing Emerging Trends:

The coffee industry, like any other, is subject to evolving trends. Staying ahead of these trends is essential for maintaining relevance and competitiveness. This section explores the current and emerging trends in the coffee market, such as the rise of specialty blends, the emphasis on sustainability, and the integration of technology in coffee services. Recognizing and adapting to these trends allows entrepreneurs to position their coffee trucks as innovative and in tune with the ever-changing preferences of the consumer base.

Analyzing Market Data:

Data is a powerful tool in making informed business decisions. Entrepreneurs must gather and analyze relevant market data to assess the viability of a coffee truck business in a specific area. This involves evaluating factors such as foot traffic, local demographics, and economic indicators. Analytical tools and methodologies, including SWOT analysis (Strengths, Weaknesses, Opportunities, Threats), can be employed to assess the internal and external factors that may impact the success of the venture. By systematically analyzing market data, entrepreneurs can identify potential challenges and opportunities, enabling them to formulate a robust business strategy.

Tools and Insights for Effective Market Research:

To guide readers through the market research process, this section provides practical tools and insights. It outlines effective survey techniques, methods for gathering observational data, and resources for accessing industry reports and market trends. Entrepreneurs will gain a clear understanding of the tools at their disposal, empowering them to conduct comprehensive market research that informs key business decisions.

Market Analysis and Trends emphasizes the indispensable nature of thorough market research before venturing into the coffee truck business. By identifying competitors, understanding customer preferences, recognizing emerging trends, and analyzing market data, entrepreneurs can make informed decisions that lay the groundwork for a successful and sustainable coffee truck enterprise.

.

Identifying Target Audience and Niche

Understanding and connecting with the right audience is fundamental to the success of any business, and the mobile coffee industry is no exception. This section delves into the significance of identifying a target audience and carving out a unique niche in the market, providing guidance on how entrepreneurs can tailor their offerings to meet specific customer preferences and create a distinctive brand identity.

Defining a Target Audience:

The first step in this process involves clearly defining the target audience. Entrepreneurs need to identify the demographics, behaviors, and psychographics of the individuals they aim to attract. This section guides readers through the development of buyer personas, detailed representations of their ideal customers. By understanding factors such as age, lifestyle, preferences, and purchasing behavior, entrepreneurs can tailor their coffee truck offerings to appeal directly to their target audience.

Understanding Customer Needs:

To build a strong and loyal customer base, entrepreneurs must go beyond demographic data and delve into the specific needs and desires of their target audience. Conducting surveys, interviews, or engaging in direct interactions allows entrepreneurs to gain insights into customer preferences regarding coffee flavors, brewing methods, and overall experiences. By aligning offerings with these needs, coffee truck businesses can create a more personalized and satisfying customer experience, fostering customer loyalty and positive word-of-mouth.

Crafting a Unique Niche:

Setting a coffee truck apart from the competition involves crafting a unique niche in the market. This could be achieved through various means, such as offering specialty coffee blends, emphasizing sustainable and ethical practices, or focusing on local and organic ingredients. Entrepreneurs are guided through the process of identifying their strengths, passions, and values to carve out a niche that aligns with their brand identity and resonates with the target audience. This distinctive positioning not only attracts customers but also establishes a memorable brand image.

Tailoring Offerings to Meet Preferences:

Once the target audience and niche are identified, entrepreneurs can tailor their coffee offerings to meet specific preferences. This involves developing a menu that reflects the tastes and values of the target demographic. Whether it's offering unique flavor combinations, accommodating dietary preferences, or providing customizable options, this section provides practical insights on how coffee truck businesses can adjust their offerings to cater to the distinct preferences of their identified audience.

Communicating the Unique Selling Proposition:

Crafting a compelling unique selling proposition (USP) is crucial for conveying the value and uniqueness of the coffee truck business to the target audience. This section explores effective ways to communicate the USP through branding, marketing messages, and visual elements. Entrepreneurs will learn how to create a brand identity that resonates with their audience and effectively communicates the reasons why their coffee truck stands out from the competition.

Identifying Target Audience and Niche highlights the pivotal role of understanding the target audience and establishing a unique niche in the mobile coffee industry. By defining a specific customer demographic, understanding their needs, crafting a distinctive niche, and tailoring offerings accordingly, entrepreneurs can create a strong foundation for a successful and differentiated coffee truck business. This strategic approach sets the stage for long-term success, as it not only attracts the right customers but also builds a loyal following that becomes the cornerstone of the venture's growth.

Chapter 2

Market Research and Planning

In the journey of launching a successful coffee truck business, this chapter serves as a crucial waypoint - the intersection where entrepreneurial dreams meet strategic reality. Market research and planning form the backbone of any thriving venture, laying the groundwork for informed decision-making. In this chapter, we will navigate through the intricate process of conducting thorough market research and developing a comprehensive business plan. From understanding the competitive landscape to projecting financial viability, each sub-chapter serves as a guidepost, offering insights that are pivotal for steering the coffee truck business towards success.

Conducting Market Research

Market research is the cornerstone of informed decision-making in the business world, providing entrepreneurs with a roadmap for success. In the dynamic landscape of the mobile coffee industry, this sub-chapter serves as a guide to conducting effective market research, offering a step-by-step approach to navigate the complexities of consumer preferences, industry trends, and competitive forces.

Defining Research Objectives:

At the outset of the market research journey, entrepreneurs must define their research objectives with precision. This step is akin to setting the coordinates on a map before embarking on a journey.

Are the objectives centered on understanding customer preferences, gaining insights into competitor strengths and weaknesses, or identifying emerging market trends?

By explicitly defining these objectives, entrepreneurs ensure that the research efforts remain focused and aligned with the strategic goals of the coffee truck business.

Understanding customer behavior, evaluating market dynamics, and gauging the competitive landscape all hinge on having clearly articulated research objectives. This section emphasizes the strategic importance of this initial step, guiding entrepreneurs to reflect on the specific information they need to gather in order to make informed decisions.

Research Methods and Tools:

With research objectives in place, entrepreneurs must navigate the diverse landscape of research methods and tools available. This sub-chapter provides a comprehensive overview of both qualitative and quantitative approaches, offering insights into their respective strengths and applications.

Qualitative Methods:

Qualitative methods, such as surveys, focus groups, and in-depth interviews, offer a nuanced understanding of customer attitudes, perceptions, and preferences. Entrepreneurs will gain insights into when and how to deploy these methods effectively, ensuring that the gathered data provides rich, contextual information.

Quantitative Approaches:

For a more structured and statistically sound analysis, quantitative approaches come into play. This includes techniques like surveys with closed-ended questions, data analysis, and statistical modeling. The sub-chapter explores the scenarios in which these approaches are most beneficial, enabling entrepreneurs to choose methods that align with their research objectives and the nature of the insights they seek.

Digital Tools and Technologies:

In the digital age, technology plays a pivotal role in enhancing the efficiency and accuracy of data collection. This sub-chapter introduces entrepreneurs to a spectrum of digital tools and technologies, from online survey platforms to data analytics software. By leveraging these tools, entrepreneurs can streamline the research process, gather real-time data, and extract meaningful insights with greater precision.

Collecting and Analyzing Data:

The heart of market research lies in the meticulous collection and analysis of data. This sub-chapter guides entrepreneurs through best practices for data collection, emphasizing the importance of accuracy and representativeness.

Best Practices for Data Collection:

Entrepreneurs will learn about effective survey design, sampling techniques, and the significance of unbiased data collection. The sub-chapter also explores the use of observational research and secondary data sources, offering a holistic approach to gathering comprehensive and reliable information.

Robust Data Analysis:

Collecting data is just the beginning; the real value lies in transforming raw data into actionable insights. This section introduces entrepreneurs to robust data analysis techniques, including SWOT analysis and competitor benchmarking. By systematically analyzing the gathered data, entrepreneurs can distill key findings that inform strategic decision-making.

Conducting Market Research provides a guide for entrepreneurs stepping into the world of the mobile coffee industry. From defining research objectives to selecting appropriate methods and tools, and finally, collecting and analyzing data, each step is critical in building a solid foundation of market intelligence. Armed with these insights, entrepreneurs are equipped to make informed decisions that will shape the success of their coffee truck business.

Analyzing Competitors and Identifying Unique Selling Points:

In the dynamic and competitive landscape of the mobile coffee industry, understanding the strengths and weaknesses of competitors is a strategic imperative. This sub-chapter is dedicated to guiding entrepreneurs through the intricacies of competitor analysis and the subsequent identification of Unique Selling Points (USPs) that will set their coffee truck apart in the market.

Competitor Identification and Profiling:

Identifying competitors goes beyond mere acknowledgment; it requires a comprehensive understanding of their operations and market positioning. Entrepreneurs should explore effective methods for identifying both direct and indirect competitors.

Direct Competitors:

Direct competitors are those offering similar products or services in the same market. Entrepreneurs will learn to identify these rivals, understanding their menu offerings, pricing strategies, and overall market share. Profiling direct competitors involves a detailed examination of factors such as customer base, geographical presence, and marketing strategies. By scrutinizing these elements, entrepreneurs can gain insights into the strengths and weaknesses that will inform their own business strategy.

Indirect Competitors:

Indirect competitors may not offer the same products but could satisfy similar consumer needs. This section explores methods for identifying indirect competitors, emphasizing the importance of a broad market perspective. Entrepreneurs will learn to recognize potential substitutes for their products and understand how these alternatives might impact their market share.

Comprehensive Competitor Profiles:

Once competitors are identified, the next step is to create comprehensive competitor profiles. This involves an in-depth analysis of their menu offerings, pricing structures, customer service practices, and overall market positioning. Entrepreneurs will gain practical insights into the methodologies for gathering this information, whether through market research, online reviews, or direct observation. These competitor profiles serve as a foundation for strategic differentiation, enabling entrepreneurs to craft a unique value proposition for their coffee truck.

SWOT Analysis:

The SWOT analysis is a powerful tool for strategic planning, providing a structured framework to assess internal strengths and weaknesses, as well as external opportunities and threats.

Strengths:

Entrepreneurs will identify and leverage internal strengths, such as unique recipes, skilled baristas, or efficient operational processes. Understanding these strengths allows for a strategic alignment with the core competencies that set the coffee truck apart in the market.

Weaknesses:

Acknowledging weaknesses is a crucial step in proactive business management. This section guides entrepreneurs in recognizing and addressing internal weaknesses, whether they pertain to operational inefficiencies, supply chain vulnerabilities, or other factors that could hinder the success of the coffee truck.

Opportunities:

By assessing external opportunities, entrepreneurs can identify avenues for growth and expansion. This sub-chapter explores how market trends, emerging consumer preferences, or untapped geographical locations can present opportunities for the coffee truck business.

Threats:

External threats, such as economic downturns, changing regulations, or increased competition, can pose challenges to the coffee truck venture. This guides entrepreneurs in developing strategies to mitigate these threats and build resilience in the face of external challenges.

Identifying Unique Selling Points (USPs):

Armed with a deep understanding of competitors and an analysis of internal and external factors, entrepreneurs can now focus on identifying and articulating their Unique Selling Points (USPs).

Leveraging Strengths:

Building on the insights gained through competitor analysis and SWOT, this section explores how to leverage internal strengths as USPs. Whether it's the use of premium coffee beans sourced from specific regions, a commitment to sustainability, or an innovative approach to customer service, entrepreneurs will learn to identify and emphasize the aspects that set their coffee truck apart.

Aligning with Customer Needs:

USPs gain their potency when they align with the needs and preferences of the target audience. This sub-chapter delves into the process of understanding customer desires and tailoring USPs to meet those needs. Whether customers value eco-friendly practices, unique flavor combinations, or personalized experiences, aligning USPs with customer preferences is key to differentiation.

Crafting a Compelling Value Proposition:

The culmination of competitor analysis and USP identification is the crafting of a compelling value proposition. Entrepreneurs will learn how to communicate their unique offerings effectively, whether through branding, marketing messages, or visual elements. A well-defined value proposition not only attracts the target audience but also forms the basis for long-term customer loyalty.

Analyzing Competitors and Identifying Unique Selling Points provides entrepreneurs in the mobile coffee industry with a strategic roadmap for differentiation. By understanding the competitive landscape, conducting a SWOT analysis, and identifying USPs, entrepreneurs can carve out a distinctive space in the market and set the stage for a successful and differentiated coffee truck business.

Creating a Business Plan with Financial Projections

With a thorough understanding of the market and a strategic differentiation plan in place, entrepreneurs are now poised to translate their vision into a tangible roadmap for success. This sub-chapter focuses on the pivotal task of creating a comprehensive business plan, with a specific emphasis on financial projections to ensure the long-term financial health of the coffee truck business.

Components of a Business Plan

A well-structured business plan serves as a guiding document that encapsulates the vision, mission, goals, and strategies of the coffee truck business. This section provides a detailed guide through each essential component of a comprehensive business plan.

Executive Summary:

The executive summary encapsulates the essence of the business plan, providing a snapshot of the venture's key components. Entrepreneurs will learn to distill their mission, target market, unique selling points, and financial goals into a concise and compelling summary.

Company Description:

Entrepreneurs will explore aspects such as the business's history, mission statement, legal structure, and location, setting the stage for a deeper understanding of the venture's identity.

Market Analysis:

Building on the market research conducted earlier, entrepreneurs will learn how to integrate key market insights into their business plan. This includes an analysis of customer demographics, industry trends, competitor positioning, and a SWOT analysis. The market analysis section forms the foundation for the subsequent strategic decisions outlined in the business plan.

Organizational Structure:

Entrepreneurs will outline the organizational structure of their coffee truck business, detailing roles and responsibilities. This section provides insights into the key team members, their qualifications, and how their skills align with the overall objectives of the business.

Marketing Plan:

The marketing plan outlines how the coffee truck will position itself in the market and attract customers. Entrepreneurs will explore strategies for branding, promotion, pricing, and customer engagement. This section serves as a roadmap for the execution of marketing initiatives that align with the overall business strategy.

Financial Projections and Budgeting:

Accurate financial projections are a cornerstone of a successful business plan, guiding entrepreneurs in securing funding and making informed financial decisions. This sub-chapter provides a deep dive into the intricacies of financial forecasting.

Revenue Projections:

Entrepreneurs will explore methodologies for projecting revenue, taking into account factors such as sales forecasts, pricing strategies, and market demand. This section provides practical tools and techniques to create realistic revenue projections that align with the overall business strategy.

Expense Budgets:

Effective budgeting is crucial for managing costs and ensuring financial sustainability. Entrepreneurs will learn how to create detailed expense budgets, accounting for fixed and variable costs, equipment purchases, operational expenses, and marketing expenditures.

Profit Margins and Financial Ratios:

Understanding profit margins and financial ratios is essential for assessing the financial health of the business. Entrepreneurs will gain insights into calculating key financial ratios and ensuring that profit margins are in line with industry standards. This section provides practical methodologies for financial analysis and decision-making.

Risk Assessment and Contingency Planning:

Every business plan must address potential risks and have a robust contingency plan in place. This sub-chapter explores common risks in the mobile coffee industry and guides entrepreneurs in developing proactive strategies to mitigate these risks.

Identifying Risks:

Entrepreneurs will learn to identify potential risks specific to the mobile coffee industry, such as weather-dependent sales, equipment breakdowns, or fluctuations in commodity prices. A comprehensive understanding of these risks forms the basis for proactive risk management.

Contingency Planning:

Developing a contingency plan involves outlining strategies to address identified risks. This section guides entrepreneurs in developing actionable contingency plans, ensuring that the coffee truck business remains resilient in the face of challenges.

This section serves as a crucial bridge between strategic planning and actionable implementation. By creating a comprehensive business plan with a focus on financial projections, entrepreneurs can confidently navigate the complexities of the mobile coffee industry. Armed with a roadmap that encapsulates their vision, mission, and financial strategies, entrepreneurs are well-positioned to turn their coffee truck dreams into a thriving reality.

Chapter 3

Setting Up Your Coffee Truck Operation

This chapter is the blueprint for setting up a seamless and successful coffee truck operation. From navigating the regulatory landscape to designing an efficient layout and sourcing quality equipment, each sub-chapter guides entrepreneurs through the intricacies of establishing a mobile coffee venture.

Regulatory Compliance and Licensing:

Embarking on the journey of a mobile coffee venture is an exciting endeavor, but navigating the intricate web of regulations governing mobile food businesses is a critical first step. This sub-chapter serves as a comprehensive guide, ensuring that the coffee truck operation not only pours delicious brews but does so within the bounds of legal requirements.

Understanding Regulatory Landscape:

The regulatory landscape for mobile food businesses encompasses a myriad of rules and regulations, from health codes to zoning laws and licensing requirements. This section immerses entrepreneurs in the complexities of these regulations, emphasizing the importance of a nuanced understanding at the local, state, and federal levels.

Health Codes:

Health codes dictate the standards for food safety and hygiene. Entrepreneurs will explore the specific health codes relevant to mobile coffee operations, covering aspects such as the cleanliness of equipment, proper food storage, and the handling of ingredients. Understanding and adhering to these codes is essential to guarantee the safety of the food and beverages served to customers.

Zoning Laws:

Zoning laws dictate where and how mobile food businesses can operate. This sub-chapter sheds light on the zoning regulations that may impact the coffee truck's choice of locations. Entrepreneurs will gain insights into identifying permissible zones, understanding restrictions, and navigating the zoning landscape to find optimal spots for their operation.

Licensing Requirements:

Beyond health and zoning regulations, specific licenses are often required for mobile food businesses. This section provides a detailed overview of the various licenses entrepreneurs need to secure. This includes mobile vending licenses, which grant permission to operate in specific areas, and food handler certifications, ensuring that staff members are trained to uphold food safety standards.

Obtaining Necessary Permits and Licenses:

Navigating the bureaucratic labyrinth of permits and licenses can be a daunting task. This sub-chapter breaks down the process into actionable steps, providing entrepreneurs with a roadmap to ensure legal compliance.

Health Permits:

Health permits are a cornerstone of mobile food businesses, and the application process varies by location. Entrepreneurs will gain practical insights into the requirements for obtaining health permits, including necessary documentation, inspections, and timelines. This section equips them with the knowledge to navigate the health permit application process smoothly.

Mobile Vending Licenses:

Securing a mobile vending license is pivotal for legal operation. From understanding local regulations to submitting required documentation, entrepreneurs will gain practical tips to streamline the licensing process and secure the necessary approvals.

Food Handler Certifications:

Ensuring that staff members are well-versed in food safety practices is crucial. This section explores the importance of food handler certifications and guides entrepreneurs on how to ensure that their team receives the necessary training. Compliance with food handler certification requirements not only upholds health standards but also builds trust with customers.

Ensuring Food Safety Compliance:

In the mobile food industry, where customers expect not only delicious but also safe food and beverages, entrepreneurs must prioritize food safety. This delves into best practices for ensuring compliance with food safety standards.

Proper Storage and Handling:

Entrepreneurs will explore guidelines for proper storage and handling of ingredients, emphasizing the importance of maintaining freshness and preventing contamination. Adhering to these practices is essential for delivering high-quality, safe products to customers.

Sanitation Procedures:

Maintaining a clean and sanitary environment is a non-negotiable aspect of food safety. From regular cleaning schedules to waste disposal practices, entrepreneurs will gain insights into creating a hygienic workspace.

Staff Training:

The human factor is critical in ensuring food safety. This underscores the importance of staff training in maintaining high standards of food safety. Entrepreneurs will learn how to develop comprehensive training programs covering hygiene practices, equipment handling, and customer interaction to ensure that every team member is a guardian of food safety.

Regulatory Compliance and Licensing is the cornerstone of a legally sound and ethically responsible mobile coffee business. By understanding the regulatory landscape, obtaining necessary permits and licenses, and prioritizing food safety compliance, entrepreneurs lay the foundation for a venture that not only satisfies taste buds but also upholds the highest standards of legality and hygiene. As the coffee truck gears up to hit the streets, entrepreneurs can move forward with confidence, knowing that their operation is not just brewing excellence but doing so within the bounds of the law and the expectations of conscientious customers.

Healthy and Safety Regulations

Health and safety regulations are a critical aspect of ensuring the well-being of individuals in various environments, including workplaces, public spaces, and establishments serving food and beverages. In the context of a mobile coffee business or any food-related venture, compliance with health and safety regulations is paramount to protect both customers and employees. Here is an overview of key health and safety regulations applicable to mobile coffee businesses:

1. Food Safety Standards:

- *HACCP (Hazard Analysis Critical Control Point):* This systematic preventive approach identifies, evaluates, and controls potential hazards in the food production process. Mobile coffee businesses must implement HACCP principles to ensure the safety of the beverages and food items they serve.

- *Safe Food Handling Practices:* Adherence to safe food handling practices is essential to prevent foodborne illnesses. This includes proper storage, cooking, and serving of food, as well as maintaining hygiene in food preparation areas.

2. Health Permits and Licensing:

- *Local Health Department Regulations:* Health permits are typically issued by local health departments, and compliance involves meeting specific criteria related to the cleanliness of the operation, proper storage of ingredients, and the overall hygiene of the food truck.

- *Food Handler Certifications*: Many jurisdictions require food handlers to undergo training and obtain certification to ensure they are knowledgeable about food safety practices.

3. Zoning and Location Compliance:

- *Zoning Regulations:* Mobile coffee businesses must comply with zoning laws to determine where they can legally operate. This includes restrictions on operating near residential areas, schools, or other businesses.

- *Permitted Operating Locations:* Identifying and adhering to permitted operating locations is crucial to avoid legal issues. Some areas may require specific permissions or agreements for mobile food businesses to operate on public or private property.

4. Occupational Health and Safety (OSHA):

- *Workplace Safety:* If the mobile coffee business has employees, it must comply with Occupational Health and Safety Administration (OSHA) standards. This includes providing a safe working environment, proper training for employees, and addressing potential hazards.

- Vehicle Safety: Ensuring the safety of the mobile coffee truck itself, including equipment installation and maintenance, is essential. This involves regular inspections, compliance with vehicle safety standards, and proper maintenance procedures.

5. Allergen Management:

- *Identification and Communication:* Mobile coffee businesses must be vigilant in identifying and communicating the presence of allergens in their products. Clear labeling and communication with customers regarding potential allergens are essential to prevent allergic reactions.

6. COVID-19 Safety Measures:

- *Pandemic Guidelines:* In light of the COVID-19 pandemic, additional health and safety measures may be required. This could include practices such as mask-wearing, social distancing, and sanitation protocols to prevent the spread of infectious diseases.

7. Emergency Preparedness:

- *First Aid and Emergency Response:* Mobile coffee businesses should have proper first aid supplies on hand and establish emergency response procedures. This includes training staff on how to handle emergencies and having a clear plan for incidents such as fires or injuries.

Compliance with health and safety regulations is not only a legal requirement but also a commitment to the well-being of both customers and staff. Regular training, monitoring, and updates to procedures are essential to adapt to changing regulations and ensure a safe and enjoyable experience for all involved in the mobile coffee business.

Permits and Licenses Required:

The aroma of freshly brewed coffee is accompanied by a web of permits and licenses that entrepreneurs must navigate. This sub-chapter serves as a compass, guiding aspiring coffee truck owners through the essential permits and licenses required to ensure a legal and compliant operation.

Understanding Permit and License Landscape

1. **Mobile Vending License:**

A Mobile Vending License grants the legal authority to operate a mobile food business, including a coffee truck, in specific areas.

- *Application Process:* Entrepreneurs will delve into the intricacies of applying for a Mobile Vending License. This involves submitting necessary documentation, which may include business registration, vehicle details, and health department approvals.

- *Navigating Local Regulations:* The sub-chapter explores the importance of understanding local regulations governing mobile vending. Entrepreneurs will gain insights into restrictions, permit fees, and the application timeline.

2. **Health Permit:**

- *Critical for Food Safety:* A Health Permit is a non-negotiable component, ensuring that the mobile coffee operation complies with health codes and standards.

- *Application Process*: Entrepreneurs will receive practical guidance on obtaining a Health Permit. This includes undergoing inspections, meeting cleanliness standards, and submitting necessary documentation.

- *Continuous Compliance:* The sub-chapter emphasizes the need for ongoing compliance, as health permits are subject to renewal and regular inspections to maintain food safety standards.

3. **Food Handler Certifications:**

- *Training for Safe Practices*: Food Handler Certifications are essential for ensuring that staff members are well-trained in safe food handling practices.

- *Training Programs:* Entrepreneurs will explore the importance of implementing comprehensive training programs for their team. This includes understanding the curriculum, conducting regular training sessions, and keeping certifications up to date.

- *Customer Assurance:* The sub-chapter highlights how food handler certifications not only uphold legal requirements but also build trust with customers who prioritize the safety of the food they consume.

Navigating the Application Process

1. Mobile Vending License Application:

- Documentation Requirements: Entrepreneurs will receive a detailed breakdown of the documentation needed for a Mobile Vending License application. This may include proof of ownership, vehicle specifications, and insurance details.

- Timelines and Processing: Understanding the timelines and processing steps involved in a mobile vending license application is crucial. The sub-chapter provides practical tips to streamline the process and expedite approvals.

2. Health Permit Application:

- Inspection Preparation: Entrepreneurs will learn how to prepare for health inspections, ensuring that their mobile coffee operation meets the necessary cleanliness and safety standards.

- Application Submission: The sub-chapter guides entrepreneurs through the steps of submitting a health permit application. This involves providing accurate information about the business, its location, and compliance with health codes.

3. Food Handler Certification Process:

- Training Providers: Entrepreneurs will explore accredited training providers for food handler certifications. This includes online courses, in-person training sessions, and resources to ensure staff members receive the necessary education.

- Renewal Procedures: Understanding the renewal procedures for food handler certifications is essential. The sub-chapter provides insights into keeping certifications up to date and compliant with regulatory requirements.

Ensuring Ongoing Compliance

1. Renewal Processes:

- *Timely Renewals:* Entrepreneurs will gain insights into the renewal processes for mobile vending licenses, health permits, and food handler certifications. Timely renewals are critical to maintaining a legally compliant operation.

- *Updates and Changes:* The sub-chapter emphasizes the need for entrepreneurs to stay informed about any updates or changes to permit and license requirements. This includes adapting to evolving regulations and ensuring continuous compliance.

2. Record-Keeping Practices:

- *Documentation Maintenance:* Entrepreneurs will learn the importance of maintaining organized records related to permits and licenses. This includes keeping track of renewal dates, inspection reports, and any correspondence with regulatory authorities.

- Audit Preparedness: The sub-chapter provides practical tips for being audit-ready, ensuring that all necessary documentation is readily available in case of inspections or inquiries.

Permits and Licenses required is the indispensable guide for entrepreneurs navigating the bureaucratic landscape of the mobile coffee industry. By understanding the intricacies of mobile vending licenses, health permits, and food handler certifications, entrepreneurs are equipped to launch and sustain a legally compliant and safe coffee truck operation. As the aroma of freshly brewed coffee wafts from the mobile coffee truck, customers can enjoy not just a delightful beverage but the assurance that it comes from a venture that prioritizes adherence to regulations and the highest standards of food safety.

Chapter 4

Setting Up Your Coffee Truck

As the wheels of ambition start turning, Chapter 4 embarks on the exciting journey of transforming a standard vehicle into a mobile haven of caffeine delights. This chapter delves into the intricacies of setting up a coffee truck, from choosing the right truck or trailer to equipping it with the finest coffee-making machinery and designing a layout that is both attractive and functionally efficient. The entrepreneurial barista is guided through each step, ensuring that every sip served on wheels is not just a beverage but an experience.

Choosing the Right Truck or Trailer: Defining Your Mobile Coffee Haven

Embarking on the journey of setting up a mobile coffee business is an exhilarating endeavor, and the choice between a truck and a trailer becomes a pivotal decision. This sub-chapter, "Defining Your Mobile Coffee Haven," meticulously guides entrepreneurs through the process of choosing the right vehicle that will not only transport them physically but also symbolically into the hearts of their caffeine-seeking clientele.

Understanding Business Needs

1. Target Audience Analysis:

- *Demographics and Preferences:* The sub-chapter initiates with a deep dive into understanding the target audience. Entrepreneurs will analyze demographics, preferences, and behavior patterns to align the mobile coffee business with the desires of their potential customers.

2. Menu Offerings Evaluation:

- *Tailoring the Experience*: Entrepreneurs will explore how the menu offerings play a pivotal role in defining the mobile coffee haven. Understanding whether the focus is on specialty brews, innovative flavors, or a streamlined selection will guide the choice of the vehicle.

3. Operational Requirements Assessment:

- *Efficiency and Workflow:* Delving into the operational needs, entrepreneurs will evaluate the requirements for efficient workflow. From storage space to equipment placement, this section sets the foundation for a seamless and functional mobile coffee operation.

Selecting the Ideal Vehicle

1. Truck vs. Trailer Considerations:

- Mobility and Flexibility: Entrepreneurs will navigate the decision-making process between a truck and a trailer. This section provides a detailed analysis of the pros and cons of each, considering factors such as mobility, maneuverability, and the ability to navigate diverse locations.

2. Size and Capacity Planning:

- *Matching Business Scale*: The sub-chapter explores the importance of size and capacity in alignment with the business scale. Entrepreneurs will learn how to select a vehicle that caters to the potential volume of customers while ensuring operational efficiency.

3. Customization Possibilities:

- *Brand Identity Integration*: Entrepreneurs will explore how the chosen vehicle can be a canvas for expressing the brand identity. Whether through branding, color schemes, or visual elements, customization possibilities are discussed to transform the vehicle into a mobile coffee haven that resonates with the target audience.

Navigating Budget Constraints

1. Balancing Quality and Cost:

 - *Pragmatic Decision-Making:* Budget considerations are an inherent part of the decision-making process. This sub-chapter provides entrepreneurs with strategies for striking a balance between the quality of the chosen vehicle and the associated costs. Practical tips on cost-effective choices without compromising on essential features are explored.

2. Negotiating and Financing Tips:

 - *Smart Negotiation Strategies*: Entrepreneurs will gain insights into negotiating with sellers or dealers to secure favorable terms. Additionally, the sub-chapter delves into exploring financing options, including loans and leasing, to make the investment in the mobile coffee haven financially viable.

Customization Possibilities

1. Transforming Standard into Special:

 - *Crafting Visual Appeal*: This section is a creative exploration into transforming a standard vehicle into a unique and visually appealing coffee haven. Entrepreneurs will learn about branding possibilities, exterior design considerations, and modifications that elevate the mobile coffee venture into a distinctive and memorable experience.

2. Exterior Design and Branding Strategies:

- *Creating Visual Identity:* Entrepreneurs will delve into the art of exterior design and branding. From logos to color schemes, this provides guidance on creating a cohesive visual identity that communicates the essence of the mobile coffee business to potential customers.

3. Functional Modifications:

- *Beyond Aesthetics:* Entrepreneurs will explore functional modifications that enhance the efficiency of the mobile coffee operation. This includes considerations for equipment placement, storage solutions, and ergonomic design to ensure a smooth workflow.

"Choosing the Right Truck or Trailer: Defining Your Mobile Coffee Haven" sets the stage for entrepreneurs to make informed decisions that go beyond the physical attributes of the vehicle. By understanding their target audience, evaluating menu offerings and operational needs, navigating the choice between a truck and a trailer, managing budget constraints, and exploring customization possibilities, entrepreneurs lay the groundwork for a mobile coffee venture that not only serves coffee but becomes a haven for enthusiasts seeking a unique and delightful experience on wheels. As the wheels of the chosen vehicle start turning, entrepreneurs are not just moving forward; they are rolling into the hearts of their customers, brewing dreams and serving up a taste of their passion for the love of coffee.

Equipping the Truck with Coffee Making Equipment: Understanding Equipment Essentials

Embarking on the caffeinated journey of a mobile coffee venture requires more than just passion – it demands a meticulous understanding of the essential coffee-making equipment that transforms a standard truck into a haven of aromatic brews. This sub-chapter, "*Understanding Equipment Essentials*," takes aspiring entrepreneurs on a detailed exploration of the key components required for a mobile coffee operation.

Identifying Key Coffee-Making Components

1. Espresso Machines:

   - *Heart of the Operation:* This initiates with the cornerstone of any coffee venture – the espresso machine. Entrepreneurs will gain insights into the types of espresso machines, understanding factors such as semi-automatic vs. automatic, volume capacity, and the role they play in crafting the perfect shot.

2. Grinders:

   - *Precision in Every Grind:* Entrepreneurs will delve into the world of grinders, understanding their crucial role in achieving the right grind size for espresso. From blade grinders to burr grinders, this section provides insights into selecting the right grinder based on quality and consistency.

3. Brewing Tools and Accessories:

- *Crafting the Perfect Cup*: Beyond the basics, entrepreneurs will explore additional brewing tools and accessories that elevate the coffee-making experience. This sub-chapter discusses the importance of items like tampers, thermometers, and scales in ensuring precision and consistency.

Sourcing Quality Coffee Machines

1. Choosing the Right Espresso Machine:

- *Factors Influencing Selection:* Entrepreneurs will navigate the decision-making process of selecting the right espresso machine. This provides in-depth insights into considerations such as volume capacity to match expected customer demand, functionality for customization, and durability for long-term reliability.

2. Exploring Machine Brands and Models:

- *Research and Recommendations*: Entrepreneurs will be guided through the process of researching and exploring various espresso machine brands and models. This sub-chapter provides practical tips on reading reviews, seeking recommendations, and making an informed decision based on the specific needs of the mobile coffee operation.

3. Cost Considerations and Budgeting:

  - *Balancing Quality and* Cost: While quality is paramount, budget considerations cannot be overlooked. This section delves into the delicate balance between choosing a high-quality espresso machine and staying within budget constraints. Practical tips on cost-effective yet reliable options are explored.

Grinders, Brewers, and More:

1. Complementary Equipment Selection:

  - *Enhancing the Coffee Arsenal*: Beyond the espresso machine, entrepreneurs will explore complementary equipment that completes the coffee arsenal. This sub-chapter guides them through the selection of grinders, brewers, and other essential tools that contribute to the diversity of the menu.

2. Evaluating Grinders:

  - *Consistency and Quality:* The focus turns to grinders, exploring the factors that contribute to consistency and quality in the grind. Entrepreneurs will understand the importance of burr grinders, dosing control, and adjusting grind settings to meet the unique requirements of different coffee offerings.

3. Brewers and Accessories:

- *Crafting Diverse Offerings:* This section delves into the world of brewers and accessories that allow entrepreneurs to craft diverse coffee offerings. From pour-over brewers to French presses and the importance of accessories like scales and timers, entrepreneurs will gain insights into enhancing their menu.

Navigating Power and Utility Requirements

1. Electrical Systems:

- *Powering the Operation:* Entrepreneurs will explore the electrical systems required to power coffee-making equipment. This sub-chapter provides insights into considerations such as voltage requirements, generator options, and electrical safety measures to ensure uninterrupted operation.

2. Water Supply and Filtration:

- *Essential for Quality Brews:* Ensuring a clean and reliable water supply is paramount in coffee-making. This section explores considerations for water tanks, water filtration systems, and the importance of maintaining water quality for the best-tasting brews.

3. Propane Usage for Mobile Operations:

- *Flexibility and Mobility:* Entrepreneurs operating mobile coffee trucks will delve into the considerations for propane usage. This sub-chapter provides insights into propane-powered espresso machines and considerations for storage and safety.

Ensuring Operational Efficiency

1. Workflow Integration:

- *Seamless Operation*: This guides entrepreneurs in integrating coffee-making equipment into the overall workflow of the mobile coffee operation. From placement strategies to ensuring ergonomic design, the goal is to create a seamless and efficient process.

2. Routine Maintenance and Cleaning:

- Sustaining Equipment Longevity: Entrepreneurs will gain insights into the importance of routine maintenance and cleaning. This sub-chapter explores best practices for keeping equipment in optimal condition, ensuring longevity and consistent performance.

In conclusion, "Equipping the Truck with Coffee Making Equipment: Understanding Equipment Essentials" is a comprehensive guide for entrepreneurs venturing into the world of mobile coffee. From the foundational components like espresso machines and grinders to the nuances of choosing the right brands, evaluating cost considerations, and navigating power and utility requirements, this sub-chapter ensures that every cup served from the mobile coffee haven is not just a beverage but a masterpiece crafted with precision and passion. As the aroma of freshly ground coffee beans fills the mobile space, entrepreneurs are equipped with the knowledge to transform their vision into a mobile coffee experience that captivates taste buds and leaves a lasting impression.

Designing an Attractive and Functional Layout: Optimizing Workflow

In the intricate dance of crafting a mobile coffee haven, the layout is the choreography that orchestrates seamless operations. This sub-chapter, "Optimizing Workflow," takes entrepreneurs on a journey of designing a layout where every movement is a step towards efficiency, ensuring that each cup of coffee is a symphony of precision and passion.

Efficiency as a Priority

1. Equipment Placement Strategies:

   - *Strategic Arrangement*: Entrepreneurs will delve into the art of placing equipment to create a flow that optimizes the coffee-making process. This provides insights into considerations such as proximity to power sources, ergonomic design, and grouping equipment for efficiency.

2. Workstation Organization:

   - *Streamlined Workflows*: This guides entrepreneurs in organizing workstations to facilitate streamlined workflows. From the espresso machine to the grinder and brewing tools, each component finds its place in a layout that minimizes unnecessary movement and maximizes efficiency.

3. Storage Solutions for Ingredients and Supplies:

- Accessible and Organized: Entrepreneurs will explore strategies for storage solutions that keep ingredients and supplies accessible and organized. This section provides insights into designing storage areas for coffee beans, syrups, and other essentials to minimize downtime during service.

Prioritizing Customer Interaction

1. Service Area Positioning:

- *Engaging Customer Experience*: Entrepreneurs will learn how to position the service area to engage customers visually and create an inviting atmosphere. This sub-chapter explores considerations for showcasing the coffee-making process and incorporating elements that make the service area a focal point.

2. Menu Displays and Information Accessibility:

- *Transparent Communication:* The sub-chapter delves into the design of menu displays and information accessibility. Entrepreneurs will explore strategies for presenting the menu clearly, incorporating visuals, and ensuring that customers can easily access information about coffee offerings.

3. Order and Pickup Points:

- *Streamlined Customer Journey*: Entrepreneurs will gain insights into positioning order and pickup points to create a streamlined customer journey. This explores the layout design to minimize wait times, enhance customer satisfaction, and create a flow that aligns with customer preferences.

Ensuring Safety and Compliance

1. Proper Storage Considerations:

- *Preserving Ingredient Quality:* This section delves into storage considerations that ensure the preservation of ingredient quality. Entrepreneurs will explore strategies for storing coffee beans, syrups, and dairy products in compliance with health and safety regulations.

2. Waste Disposal Systems:

- *Hygienic and Efficient:* Entrepreneurs will gain insights into designing waste disposal systems that are both hygienic and efficient. This sub-chapter explores considerations for waste segregation, disposal containers, and regular maintenance to meet regulatory standards.

3. Hygiene Practices and Cleaning Stations:

- *Maintaining a Clean Environment:* This guides entrepreneurs in incorporating hygiene practices and cleaning stations into the layout. From hand washing stations to designated areas for cleaning equipment, this section ensures that the mobile coffee haven maintains a clean and compliant environment.

Adapting to Limited Space

1. Compact Equipment Choices:

- *Maximizing Functionality*: Entrepreneurs operating in limited spaces will explore the art of choosing compact equipment that maximizes functionality. This provides practical tips on selecting space-efficient espresso machines, grinders, and brewing tools.

2. Creative Storage Solutions:

- *Innovative Utilization of Space:* Entrepreneurs will gain insights into creative storage solutions that make the most of every inch in a limited space. This section explores options such as built-in storage, foldable shelves, and multi-functional design elements.

3. Flexibility in Layout Design:

- Adaptable Configurations: The sub-chapter emphasizes the importance of flexibility in layout design. Entrepreneurs will explore strategies for creating adaptable configurations that can be customized based on the specific requirements of different locations and events.

"Designing an Attractive and Functional Layout: Optimizing Workflow" is the blueprint for entrepreneurs seeking to create a mobile coffee haven that is both efficient and inviting. From strategically placing equipment to prioritizing customer interaction, ensuring safety and compliance, and adapting to limited space, every element of the layout is designed with a purpose. As the wheels of the mobile coffee truck roll into various locations, the optimized layout becomes the stage where each performance is a testament to the commitment to quality, efficiency, and an unforgettable customer experience. The layout is not just a design; it's the rhythm that turns every visit to the mobile coffee haven into a harmonious blend of flavor and function.

Chapter 5

Sourcing Quality Coffee Beans and Supplies

This chapter unfolds as a journey into the heart of the operation – the sourcing of quality coffee beans and supplies. Like a maestro selecting the finest notes for a symphony, entrepreneurs must carefully curate the elements that will define the taste and essence of their offerings. This chapter, a melodic ode to quality, explores the nuances of establishing relationships with coffee suppliers, ensuring freshness and quality, and mastering the delicate art of managing inventory and supplies.

Establishing Relationships with Coffee Suppliers

Tracing the Journey: Understanding the Coffee Supply Chain

The journey of a coffee bean from the lush fields where it is cultivated to the moment it graces the cup is an intricate tapestry woven through the coffee supply chain. This sub-chapter unravels the layers of complexity, guiding entrepreneurs through the journey and highlighting the critical factors that influence the quality of the final brew.

1. The Origin of Beans:

- *Birthplace of Flavor*: Entrepreneurs will explore the origins of coffee beans, understanding how factors like altitude, climate, and soil contribute to the distinct flavors of different coffee varieties. This section emphasizes the importance of tracing the origin of beans to ensure a unique and high-quality offering.

2. Harvesting and Processing:

- *Crafting the Bean*: Delving into the harvesting and processing stages, entrepreneurs will gain insights into how the meticulous methods employed by coffee farmers' impact the final product. Understanding the nuances of wet processing, dry processing, and the timing of harvesting becomes crucial in maintaining quality.

3. Transportation and Storage:

- *Preserving Freshness:* The sub-chapter explores the transportation and storage phase, shedding light on the challenges of maintaining freshness during transit. Entrepreneurs will learn about the importance of climate-controlled shipping and storage conditions to prevent degradation of flavor.

4. Roasting and Packaging:

- The Transformative Roast: Entrepreneurs will delve into the role of roasting in shaping the flavor profile of coffee beans. This section explores different roasting techniques and how the timing and temperature of the roast impact the final taste. Packaging considerations, including the type of bag and storage recommendations, are also covered.

From Bean to Brew: Researching and Identifying Potential Suppliers

The quest for quality begins with identifying suppliers who share the same passion for exceptional coffee. This section provides entrepreneurs with a roadmap for navigating the vast landscape of potential partners, each contributing a unique note to the symphony of the coffee supply chain.

1. Local Roasters:

   - *Community Connection*: Entrepreneurs will explore the benefits of sourcing from local roasters. This sub-chapter discusses the advantages of building a connection with the local community, supporting small businesses, and ensuring a fresher supply chain due to reduced shipping distances.

2. Direct Relationships with Coffee Farmers:

   - *Fostering Direct Connections:* Entrepreneurs will be guided through the process of establishing direct relationships with coffee farmers. This section explores the advantages of bypassing intermediaries, fostering transparency, and supporting farmers in maintaining sustainable and ethical practices.

3. Collaborations with Reputable Distributors:

- *Efficiency and Expertise:* The sub-chapter delves into the option of collaborating with reputable distributors. Entrepreneurs will explore the advantages of working with distributors who bring expertise in sourcing, logistics, and quality control, ensuring a reliable and efficient supply chain.

Beyond Flavor: Building Sustainable and Ethical Partnerships

The aroma of a perfect cup extends beyond its flavor, encompassing the ethical and sustainable practices embraced by the coffee supply chain. This sub-chapter emphasizes the responsibility entrepreneurs hold in shaping a supply chain that goes beyond transactions, contributing positively to both people and the planet.

1. Supporting Fair Trade Practices:

- *Empowering Communities*: Entrepreneurs will explore the significance of supporting fair trade practices. This section discusses the positive impact of fair trade certifications, ensuring that coffee is sourced ethically, and the communities involved in its production are empowered and treated equitably.

2. Environmentally Friendly Sourcing:

- *Sustainability as a Priority:* The sub-chapter delves into the importance of environmentally friendly sourcing. Entrepreneurs will learn about sustainable farming practices, certifications such as Rainforest Alliance, and the role of their choices in minimizing the environmental footprint of their coffee supply.

3. Fostering Long-Term Relationships:

  - *Beyond Transactions*: Entrepreneurs will gain insights into the value of fostering long-term relationships with suppliers. This section emphasizes the benefits of stability, consistent quality, and mutual growth that come from partnerships built on trust and shared values.

Striking the Right Chord: Negotiating Terms and Agreements

In the intricate dance of establishing supplier relationships, negotiation becomes the rhythm that sets the tone for a mutually beneficial partnership. This sub-chapter provides entrepreneurs with the tools to navigate negotiations, ensuring that the partnership strikes the right chord for both parties.

1. Establishing Favorable Terms:

  - *Mutual Benefit*: Entrepreneurs will learn how to negotiate terms that align with the goals of both parties. This section explores considerations such as payment terms, order quantities, and exclusivity agreements, ensuring a balance that fosters a positive and sustainable relationship.

2. Pricing Structures and Transparency:

- *Clarity in Pricing:* This delves into pricing structures and the importance of transparency in negotiations. Entrepreneurs will gain insights into understanding cost breakdowns, negotiating fair prices, and establishing clear communication channels to avoid misunderstandings.

3. Ensuring a Mutually Beneficial Partnership:

- Symbiosis in Business: Entrepreneurs will explore the concept of a mutually beneficial partnership. This section emphasizes the importance of ensuring that both parties derive value from the relationship, fostering a collaborative spirit that extends beyond the transactional aspect.

In conclusion, *"Establishing Relationships with Coffee Suppliers"* is the overture to a symphony of quality and ethical practices in the mobile coffee venture. From understanding the intricate journey of coffee beans through the supply chain to researching potential suppliers, building sustainable partnerships, and striking the right chords in negotiations, entrepreneurs are equipped with the knowledge to curate a coffee experience that transcends the cup. As the journey unfolds, every sip becomes not just a flavor but a story, a narrative woven through the relationships with suppliers who share the same commitment to excellence and ethical practices. The chapter sets the stage for a coffee culture that extends beyond the mobile haven and into the hearts of those who cherish the art of a perfect brew.

Ensuring Freshness and Quality

The Essence of Aroma: Importance of Freshness in Coffee

In the aromatic realm of coffee, freshness is the heartbeat that animates every cup. This sub-chapter unfurls the importance of freshness, immersing entrepreneurs in the essence of aroma and elucidating why it stands as a non-negotiable pillar in the quest for sourcing quality coffee beans.

1. The Timeless Impact of Freshness:

   - *A Symphony in Every Sip:* Entrepreneurs will delve into the timeless impact of freshness on the coffee experience. This section explores how the moment beans are roasted, they embark on a journey of degassing, where carbon dioxide is released. Understanding this process becomes pivotal in preserving the subtle flavors and aromas that define a premium cup.

2. Direct Impact on Flavor Profile:

   - *From Bean to Cup:* The sub-chapter emphasizes the direct impact of freshness on the flavor profile of coffee. Entrepreneurs will explore how the degassing process, which occurs most prominently in the days following roasting, influences the extraction of flavors during brewing. The result is a cup that resonates with the vibrant notes of the coffee bean.

3. Customer Experience as a Priority:

- *Crafting Memories*: Entrepreneurs will be guided to perceive freshness not just as a technical aspect but as an integral part of the customer experience. This section explores how the aroma of freshly ground coffee and the nuanced flavors of a recently roasted batch create an immersive experience, crafting memories for coffee enthusiasts.

4. The Perils of Stale Coffee:

- *The Silent Foe:* The sub-chapter unravels the perils of serving stale coffee. Entrepreneurs will gain insights into how prolonged exposure to air and light accelerates the staling process, diminishing the vibrancy of flavors. Recognizing the signs of stale coffee becomes essential to maintain the integrity of the coffee experience.

Beyond the Bean: Quality Considerations in Coffee Selection

Quality in coffee transcends mere appearance; it encompasses a symphony of factors that defines its character. This section guides entrepreneurs through the multifaceted considerations that elevate a coffee bean beyond its basic attributes, ensuring that every selection aligns harmoniously with their brand identity.

1. Beyond the Bean Variety:

- *Varietal Nuances:* Entrepreneurs will explore considerations beyond the varietal aspect of coffee beans. This sub-chapter delves into how factors like altitude, climate, and soil contribute to the unique characteristics of coffee from different regions. Understanding these nuances empowers entrepreneurs to curate a diverse and exceptional selection.

2. Growing Conditions and Terroir:

- *The Essence of Terroir*: The sub-chapter unravels the influence of growing conditions and terroir on coffee quality. Entrepreneurs will gain insights into how factors like rainfall, temperature, and the overall environment shape the flavor profile. The concept of terroir, borrowed from the world of wine, becomes a guiding principle in selecting beans with distinct regional identities.

3. Processing Methods and Impact:

- *Crafting Flavor:* Entrepreneurs will delve into the world of processing methods and their impact on flavor. This section explores the differences between wet and dry processing, natural and washed methods, guiding entrepreneurs to select beans that align with the flavor profiles they aim to offer in their mobile coffee haven.

4. Certifications and Ethical Considerations:

- *Beyond Taste:* The sub-chapter expands the scope to certifications and ethical considerations. Entrepreneurs will explore how certifications like Rainforest Alliance and Fair Trade not only vouch for quality but also signify commitment to ethical and sustainable practices. This section emphasizes the role of conscious choices in shaping a responsible coffee supply chain.

The Palate as a Guide: Cupping and Tasting Sessions

In the journey to ensure quality, entrepreneurs embark on a sensory exploration through cupping and tasting sessions. This sub-chapter introduces these sessions as invaluable tools, turning the palate into a guide that navigates the nuanced world of flavors, aromas, and textures.

1. Understanding Cupping Sessions:

- *The Art of Evaluation:* Entrepreneurs will gain insights into the art of cupping sessions. This section explores the structured process of evaluating coffee, from fragrance and aroma assessment to flavor profiling. Cupping becomes a ritual where entrepreneurs fine-tune their senses to discern subtle differences in quality.

2. Training the Palate:

- *A Journey of Sensitivity:* The sub-chapter guides entrepreneurs in training their palate to become a sensitive instrument in the pursuit of quality. Engaging in regular cupping sessions hones the ability to detect flavor nuances, recognize defects, and make informed decisions about the beans that will grace their mobile coffee haven.

3. Tasting Sessions for Customer Preferences:

- *Connecting with Preferences:* Entrepreneurs will explore the extension of tasting sessions to understanding customer preferences. This section emphasizes the role of engaging customers in the tasting process, creating a dialogue about flavors, and tailoring offerings to align with the diverse palate of their clientele.

4. Continuous Improvement through Feedback:

- *Feedback as a Catalyst:* The sub-chapter delves into the role of feedback from cupping and tasting sessions as a catalyst for continuous improvement. Entrepreneurs will learn how customer input and internal evaluations shape the evolving selection of coffee beans, ensuring a dynamic and responsive approach to maintaining quality.

Preserving Perfection: Managing Storage and Shelf Life

Once the perfect beans are identified, the responsibility shifts to preserving their perfection. This section provides entrepreneurs with insights into the delicate art of managing the storage of coffee beans, ensuring that every cup poured is a testament to the peak of quality.

1. Packaging Considerations:

- *Guardians of Freshness*: Entrepreneurs will explore the role of packaging as the guardian of freshness. This sub-chapter provides insights into the importance of selecting packaging that protects beans from exposure to air, light, and moisture, preserving their aroma and flavor.

2. Storage Conditions for Prolonged Freshness:

- *Creating a Sanctuary:* The sub-chapter delves into the creation of an ideal storage environment. Entrepreneurs will gain practical tips on maintaining consistent temperature and humidity levels, avoiding exposure to strong odors, and establishing a sanctuary where beans remain at the peak of freshness.

3. Shelf Life Management Strategies:

- *A Dance with Time*: Entrepreneurs will explore strategies for managing shelf life without compromising quality. This section provides insights into considerations such as inventory turnover rates, ensuring a steady flow of fresh beans, and avoiding the pitfalls of overstocking that may lead to staleness.

4. Regular Quality Checks and Monitoring:

- *Vigilance as a Virtue:* The sub-chapter emphasizes the importance of regular quality checks and monitoring. Entrepreneurs will learn how to implement systems for tracking the freshness of their coffee inventory, conducting periodic assessments, and intervening proactively to address any deviations from the desired quality.

In conclusion, *"Ensuring Freshness and Quality" is* the symphony of meticulous curation, where every note and nuance contributes to the sensory journey of coffee enthusiasts. From understanding the essence of freshness and its impact on the customer experience to exploring the multifaceted considerations in selecting quality coffee beans, engaging in cupping and tasting sessions, and mastering the delicate art of preserving perfection through storage, entrepreneurs are equipped to orchestrate a coffee haven that resonates with excellence. As the chapter unfolds, freshness becomes more than a characteristic; it becomes a commitment, a promise to deliver a cup that embodies the vibrancy and authenticity of quality coffee. The mobile coffee haven emerges not just as a destination for a caffeine fix but as a sanctuary where every sip is a celebration of the artistry that goes into ensuring freshness and quality.

Managing Inventory and Supplies

Balancing Act: Strategic Inventory Planning

In the intricate dance of a mobile coffee venture, strategic inventory planning emerges as the choreographer, orchestrating a delicate balance between a steady supply of coffee beans and the imperative to minimize waste. This sub-chapter guides entrepreneurs through the nuances of this balancing act, exploring inventory turnover rates, forecasting methods, and considerations for managing seasonal variations.

1. Understanding Inventory Turnover Rates:

- *The Rhythm of Business:* Entrepreneurs will delve into the concept of inventory turnover rates as the heartbeat of their business. This section explores how understanding the frequency at which inventory is replenished provides insights into consumption patterns, enabling entrepreneurs to align their procurement strategies with the dynamic nature of the mobile coffee operation.

2. Forecasting Methods for Accuracy:

- *Peering into the Future:* The sub-chapter provides insights into forecasting methods as the crystal ball guiding inventory planning. Entrepreneurs will explore quantitative and qualitative approaches to forecasting demand, leveraging historical data, market trends, and customer preferences to anticipate the ebb and flow of coffee consumption.

3. Managing Seasonal Variations:

- *Adapting to Nature's Rhythms:* Entrepreneurs will navigate the nuances of managing inventory during seasonal variations. This section explores the impact of factors like weather, events, and holidays on coffee consumption patterns, guiding entrepreneurs in adapting their inventory planning to meet the unique demands of each season.

Partners in Consistency: Developing Supplier Relationships for Reliability

In the tapestry of a reliable inventory, strong relationships with suppliers stand as the threads that weave consistency. This section explores the symbiotic partnership between entrepreneurs and suppliers, emphasizing communication strategies, collaborative demand forecasting, and the creation of a flexible supply chain.

1. Effective Communication Strategies:

- *Building Bridges:* Entrepreneurs will gain insights into effective communication strategies that lay the foundation for a strong supplier relationship. This sub-chapter explores transparent and open communication channels, fostering a collaborative environment where both parties share insights, challenges, and innovations.

2. Collaborative Demand Forecasting:

- *Anticipating Together:* The sub-chapter delves into the collaborative aspect of demand forecasting. Entrepreneurs will explore how involving suppliers in the forecasting process enhances accuracy, reduces the risk of stock outs or overstocking, and creates a dynamic supply chain that adapts seamlessly to the evolving needs of the mobile coffee business.

3. Creating a Responsive Supply Chain:

- *Adapting to Changes:* Entrepreneurs will navigate the concept of a responsive supply chain. This section provides insights into strategies for creating agility in the supply chain, ensuring that it can adapt to changes in demand, unexpected events, and the dynamic nature of the mobile coffee operation.

Seamless Operations: Efficient Supply Chain Management

In the bustling world of mobile coffee, efficiency in supply chain management becomes the backbone of seamless operations. This sub-chapter provides entrepreneurs with strategies for streamlining the procurement process, minimizing lead times, and creating a supply chain that mirrors the agility and responsiveness required for success.

1. Streamlining Procurement Process:

- *Efficiency as a Virtue:* Entrepreneurs will explore the art of streamlining the procurement process. This section delves into strategies for optimizing order processes, leveraging technology for efficient communication with suppliers, and establishing protocols that minimize bureaucratic hurdles in obtaining inventory.

2. Minimizing Lead Times:

- *Time as a Currency:* Entrepreneurs will gain insights into the importance of minimizing lead times in a mobile coffee operation. This sub-chapter explores strategies for reducing the time between placing an order and receiving inventory, ensuring that the supply chain aligns with the fast-paced nature of the business.

3. Technology Integration for Efficiency:

- *Innovation in Operations:* The sub-chapter delves into the integration of technology for enhanced efficiency. Entrepreneurs will explore the role of technology in automating procurement processes, tracking inventory levels in real-time, and utilizing data analytics for informed decision-making in supply chain management.

Environmental Consciousness: Waste Reduction and Sustainability Practices

In the pursuit of an efficient inventory, environmental consciousness becomes the compass guiding entrepreneurs towards waste reduction and sustainability. This section explores strategies for minimizing waste, repurposing by-products, and integrating sustainability practices into the entire supply chain.

1. Minimizing Waste in Procurement:

- *A Greener Approach:* Entrepreneurs will explore strategies for minimizing waste at the procurement stage. This sub-chapter delves into considerations such as ordering quantities that align with demand, implementing just-in-time inventory practices, and avoiding overstocking that may lead to unnecessary waste.

2. Repurposing By-Products:

- *Creativity in Sustainability:* The sub-chapter guides entrepreneurs in exploring creative ways to repurpose by-products. From using coffee grounds for composting or beauty products to finding innovative solutions for packaging materials, entrepreneurs will gain insights into transforming waste into resources.

3. Integrating Sustainability into the Supply Chain:

- *A Holistic Approach:* The section emphasizes the importance of integrating sustainability practices into the entire supply chain. Entrepreneurs will explore considerations such as selecting eco-friendly packaging, supporting suppliers with sustainable practices, and fostering a culture of environmental consciousness throughout the mobile coffee operation.

In conclusion, "*Managing Inventory and Supplies*" emerges as the strategic orchestrator, seamlessly weaving together the threads of inventory planning, supplier relationships, efficient supply chain management, and environmental consciousness. From maintaining a delicate balance in inventory turnover rates to developing reliable supplier relationships, streamlining operations, and embracing sustainability practices, entrepreneurs are equipped with the tools to navigate the intricacies of managing inventory in the dynamic world of mobile coffee. As the chapter unfolds, it becomes evident that managing inventory is not just a logistical task but a strategic dance, where every move is calibrated to ensure a harmonious and efficient supply chain. The mobile coffee haven, guided by these principles, becomes not just a destination for a delightful cup but a testament to the commitment to excellence in every aspect of the business.

Chapter 6

Building an Online and Offline Presence

In the digital age, where the aroma of coffee meets the virtual realm, building an online and offline presence becomes the canvas upon which the mobile coffee haven paints its identity. This chapter unfolds as a symphony of creating a brand identity, developing a mobile-friendly website and social media presence, and implementing marketing strategies that echo the heartbeat of local communities.

Creating a Brand Identity

Building a brand is a nuanced art, a careful blend of storytelling, visual aesthetics, and values that resonate with the audience. In the realm of a mobile coffee business, crafting a brand identity goes beyond the mere act of serving coffee; it is about creating an immersive experience that extends beyond the beans. This sub-chapter delves into the intricacies of defining the brand essence, crafting a memorable brand name and logo, establishing brand colors and visual elements, creating a consistent brand voice, and fostering brand consistency across touch points.

1. *Defining the Brand Essence: Beyond the Beans*

Embarking on the journey of defining the brand essence is akin to discovering the soul of the mobile coffee haven. Entrepreneurs are encouraged to delve into the core values, mission, and vision that form the heartbeat of their brand. This section becomes a compass guiding every decision and action, from the selection of coffee beans to the design of the truck or trailer. Understanding the essence of the brand transforms the mobile coffee business from a mere provider of beverages into a curator of experiences, aligning every aspect with the brand's fundamental identity.

2. *Crafting a Memorable Brand Name and Logo: Symbols that Speak*

The brand name and logo become the visual and auditory anchors of the mobile coffee business. Crafting a memorable brand name involves a strategic dance between resonance and uniqueness. Entrepreneurs are guided through strategies that go beyond mere descriptors, aiming to tell a story or evoke emotions related to the brand essence. Simultaneously, designing a logo becomes an art form where symbols, colors, and shapes intertwine to encapsulate the spirit of the mobile coffee business. The brand name becomes a narrative, and the logo transforms into its visual anthem, creating a recognizable identity that echoes in the minds of customers.

3. *Establishing Brand Colors and Visual Elements: Visual Harmony*

In the world of brand identity, color is not just a visual element; it is a language. Entrepreneurs dive into the realm of color psychology, exploring the emotions and associations that different colors evoke. Selecting brand colors becomes a strategic decision, aligning with the desired brand personality and resonating with the target audience. Visual elements, from font choices to design motifs, harmonize with the overall brand identity, creating a visual language that silently communicates the essence of the mobile coffee haven. This section guides entrepreneurs in painting a canvas that visually narrates the story they want to tell.

4. *Creating a Consistent Brand Voice: Words that Whisper*

The brand voice is the storyteller in the digital and physical spaces where the mobile coffee business unfolds. Entrepreneurs are guided in creating a consistent brand voice that extends beyond marketing materials to permeate social media posts, customer interactions, and promotional content. Tone, language, and messaging become the threads of a narrative that align with the brand's personality, fostering a connection with customers. This section emphasizes the importance of words that resonate, creating an auditory experience that complements the visual identity, ensuring that the brand speaks with a unified voice across all channels.

5. *Fostering Brand Consistency across Touch points: A Unified Symphony*

Brand consistency is the glue that binds the diverse touch points of the mobile coffee business into a unified symphony. Entrepreneurs explore strategies to ensure that the brand identity remains cohesive in physical spaces, online platforms, and promotional materials. From the design of the coffee truck or trailer to the layout of the mobile-friendly website and social media profiles, every touch point becomes an opportunity to reinforce the brand's narrative. Consistency becomes the thread weaving through the customer's journey, creating a seamless and immersive brand experience.

In conclusion, the sub-chapter on creating a brand identity is a roadmap for entrepreneurs in the mobile coffee business to navigate the intricate landscape of storytelling, visuals, and values. It underscores the significance of going beyond the beans to define the essence of the brand, crafting a memorable name and logo, selecting colors and visual elements that resonate, developing a consistent brand voice, and ensuring uniformity across touch points. As the sub-chapter unfolds, entrepreneurs are equipped to not only serve a cup of coffee but to curate an experience that aligns with the soul of their brand, fostering connections that go beyond transactions. The brand identity becomes a living entity, evolving with the heartbeat of the mobile coffee haven, inviting customers to be part of a narrative that transcends the ordinary.

Developing a Mobile-Friendly Website and Social Media Presence

In the interconnected realms of the digital and physical, the mobile coffee business extends its reach through a mobile-friendly website and a vibrant social media presence. This sub-chapter serves as a compass for entrepreneurs, guiding them through the intricacies of crafting a digital identity that mirrors the warmth and authenticity of the physical coffee experience.

1. *Building a User-Friendly and Mobile-Optimized Website: The Digital Welcome Mat*

The digital welcome mat is laid out as entrepreneurs delve into the essentials of building a user-friendly website. This section emphasizes the importance of creating an experience that extends a warm welcome to online visitors, akin to the inviting aroma of coffee wafting through the air. Entrepreneurs gain insights into optimizing the website for mobile users, ensuring a seamless and accessible digital journey. The website, in essence, becomes the virtual door to the mobile coffee haven, inviting visitors to step into a world where every click is a step closer to a delightful cup of coffee.

2. *Crafting Engaging Content: Stories in a Cup*

The narrative of the mobile coffee journey comes alive through the art of crafting engaging content. Entrepreneurs are guided in storytelling, using captivating images, compelling descriptions of coffee offerings, and interactive elements that invite online visitors to immerse themselves in the rich narrative. Each image becomes a brushstroke painting the canvas of the coffee experience, and each description is a chapter in the story of the mobile coffee haven. Crafting engaging content becomes a means of not just selling coffee but inviting customers to be part of a narrative that transcends the transactional.

3. *Leveraging Social Media Platforms: Virtual Conversations*

Social media platforms emerge as dynamic hubs for virtual conversations, and entrepreneurs navigate this landscape with strategic intent. This section explores the varied platforms available, each offering a unique space for expression. From Instagram's visual allure to Twitter's concise conversations, entrepreneurs gain insights into selecting and leveraging platforms that align with their target audience. The social media presence becomes an extension of the brand personality, where every post, tweet, or image is a brushstroke contributing to the larger portrait of the mobile coffee identity.

4. *Building a Content Calendar and Posting Schedule: Consistency in Cyberspace*

In the digital realm, consistency is the heartbeat that sustains the connection with online communities. Entrepreneurs delve into the importance of creating a content calendar and posting schedule that ensures a regular and engaging flow of content. Just as the daily grind produces the perfect cup of coffee, a consistent posting schedule ensures that the digital space is alive with the aroma of the mobile coffee haven. The content calendar becomes a strategic roadmap, guiding entrepreneurs to curate a narrative that evolves seamlessly over time.

5. *Engaging with the Online Community: Digital Handshakes*

Engaging with the online community is more than just responding to comments; it's a digital handshake that fosters connections.

Entrepreneurs explore the art of building a digital rapport with followers, responding to comments, fostering conversations, and creating a sense of community. Engaging with the online community becomes a reflection of the warm hospitality offered in the physical space of the mobile coffee haven. Each response is a gesture, and every interaction is a moment where the digital and physical worlds converge.

As the sub-chapter unfolds, developing a mobile-friendly website and a vibrant social media presence emerges not just as a marketing strategy but as an extension of the mobile coffee experience. From crafting an inviting digital welcome mat to narrating stories through engaging content, leveraging social media platforms, maintaining consistency, and engaging with the online community, entrepreneurs are equipped to create a seamless and immersive online presence. The virtual and physical realms intertwine, ensuring that the aroma of the mobile coffee haven permeates the digital landscape, inviting customers to not just savor a cup of coffee but to be part of a dynamic and interactive journey. In the realm of the mobile coffee business, the online presence becomes more than a storefront; it becomes a digital haven where the essence of coffee is celebrated, and connections are brewed.

Implementing Marketing Strategies for Local Presence

In the heartbeat of local communities, the mobile coffee haven finds its rhythm. This sub-chapter unfolds as a guide, not just to marketing strategies, but to the art of building a resonance with the local ethos. It's about creating a bridge between the physical and virtual realms, where marketing becomes a means of weaving a strong and enduring presence deeply rooted in the local tapestry.

1. *Understanding the Local Landscape: Roots in the Community*

The journey begins by understanding the local landscape. Entrepreneurs delve into the demographics, preferences, and cultural nuances of the community. This section becomes a compass, guiding strategies based on the intricacies of the local ethos. From the timing of the morning rush to the preferred flavors of the community, every detail becomes a thread woven into the marketing strategy. Understanding the local landscape is not just about selling coffee; it's about becoming an integral part of the community's daily rhythm.

2. *Collaborating with Local Influencers and Businesses: Community Alliances*

The strength of the mobile coffee haven lies in community alliances. Entrepreneurs are guided in forging partnerships with local influencers and businesses. This collaboration extends the reach of the mobile coffee business beyond its wheels. From partnering with local artists to collaborating with nearby businesses, each alliance becomes a testament to community connection. The mobile coffee business is not just a vendor; it's a participant in the local narrative, aligning with the tastes and preferences that define the community.

3. *Hosting Events and Pop-Ups: Physical Touch points*

The tangible presence of events and pop-ups becomes a cornerstone of local marketing. Entrepreneurs gain insights into creating physical touch points that bring the mobile coffee experience directly to the community. From coffee tastings that awaken the senses to themed pop-ups that add a touch of novelty, each event becomes an opportunity for face-to-face engagement. In a world inundated with digital noise, the physical touch points become moments where the community can not only taste the coffee but feel the heartbeat of the mobile coffee haven.

4. *Implementing Loyalty Programs and Local Discounts: Nurturing Relationships*

Nurturing relationships takes center stage as entrepreneurs delve into implementing loyalty programs and local discounts. Strategies are explored for creating incentives that go beyond transactions. Whether it's a punch card for free coffee after a certain number of purchases or exclusive discounts for local residents, loyalty becomes a reciprocal bond. The mobile coffee business is not just a fleeting vendor; it's a local companion, rewarding loyalty and fostering a sense of belonging within the community.

5. *Monitoring and Adapting Marketing Strategies: Agility in Action*

In the dynamic dance of local marketing, agility becomes the key. Entrepreneurs navigate the changing landscape by monitoring the effectiveness of campaigns, analyzing customer feedback, and adapting strategies based on real-time insights. The mobile coffee business is not static; it's a living entity that evolves with the pulse of the local community. Agility ensures that marketing strategies remain attuned to the evolving needs and preferences of the community, fostering a connection that is not just sustained but thrives over time.

As the sub-chapter concludes, implementing marketing strategies for local presence is not just a strategy; it's an art form. It's about understanding the local landscape, forging alliances, creating physical touch points, nurturing relationships, and embracing agility. The mobile coffee business doesn't just serve coffee; it becomes a part of the local story, a chapter in the community's narrative. Marketing becomes a means of not just promoting a product but of building a relationship with the local community, where every cup served is a testament to the enduring presence of the mobile coffee haven in the hearts of its patrons.

Chapter 7

Providing Excellent Customer Service

In the aromatic realm of the mobile coffee haven, customer service emerges as the heartbeat, beating in rhythm with the desires and expectations of patrons. This chapter unfolds as a guide to cultivating an exceptional customer experience, exploring the nuances of staff training, loyalty programs, and responsive feedback mechanisms.

Training Staff for Customer Interaction - Brewing Interpersonal Excellence

In the symphony of the mobile coffee experience, the staff takes center stage as the orchestrators of customer interaction. This sub-chapter delves into the art of training staff for excellence in customer service.

Understanding the Art of Hospitality

In the intimate dance between a customer and a mobile coffee haven, staff members play the role of ambassadors, breathing life into the concept of hospitality. Entrepreneurs guide their staff not only to serve coffee but to create an atmosphere where every interaction is a moment of warmth and positive memory for the customer.

Understanding the art of hospitality goes beyond the mechanics of brewing coffee. It involves instilling a genuine desire to enhance the customer's experience. Staff members are encouraged to view themselves as hosts, welcoming guests into a comforting and inviting space. This mindset shift sets the tone for a service culture that prioritizes the emotional connection between staff and customers.

From the warm greeting when a customer approaches the mobile coffee haven to the attentive farewell as they take their leave, staff members are coached to embody hospitality at every touch point. The goal is to make the customer feel not just like a patron but a welcomed guest, creating a memorable experience that transcends the transaction.

Effective Communication Skills

Communication is the lifeblood of exceptional customer service. Entrepreneurs recognize that effective communication is more than just exchanging pleasantries; it's about creating a meaningful dialogue. Staff members are equipped with the skills to engage customers warmly, making each interaction a genuine exchange rather than a transactional process.

Training in effective communication involves various elements. From body language to verbal tone, staff members learn to convey a sense of approachability and friendliness. The importance of active listening is emphasized, ensuring that customers feel heard and valued. Clear and concise communication about menu offerings, specials, and brewing methods becomes a crucial aspect of the training.

The menu, with its array of coffee choices, becomes a canvas for communication. Staff members are coached to guide customers through the options, explaining the flavor profiles, suggesting pairings, and even recommending based on individual preferences. This not only enhances the customer's understanding of the offerings but also personalizes the experience, fostering a sense of connection.

Product Knowledge and Recommendations

Staff members are not merely servers; they are coffee connoisseurs navigating the intricate world of blends, brewing methods, and flavor profiles. The sub-chapter focuses on transforming staff into knowledgeable guides who can enrich the customer's journey through the diverse landscape of coffee offerings.

Entrepreneurs recognize that a well-informed staff is essential for elevating the customer experience. Training involves comprehensive education on the coffee menu, delving into the origin of the beans, the nuances of different brewing methods, and the distinctive flavor notes of each blend. This knowledge empowers staff members to engage in informative conversations with customers, answering queries and providing insights.

Leveraging product knowledge to make personalized recommendations becomes an art form. Staff members are encouraged to understand customer preferences, whether it's a preference for bold and robust flavors or a penchant for subtle and nuanced profiles. Through thoughtful suggestions, staff members can guide customers to explore new blends, creating a personalized and memorable tasting experience.

Resolving Customer Issues:

In the dynamic realm of customer service, challenges may arise, and this sub-chapter guides staff members in the art of effective issue resolution. The focus is not just on problem-solving but on transforming issues into opportunities to showcase exceptional service.

Training in issue resolution begins with instilling a mindset of empathy. Staff members are encouraged to view customer concerns as legitimate and valid, irrespective of the scale of the issue. This empathetic approach lays the foundation for a positive resolution process.

The sub-chapter explores specific strategies for handling various customer issues, from minor inconveniences to more complex problems. Staff members are equipped with effective communication techniques to de-escalate tense situations, turning potential conflicts into opportunities for understanding and collaboration.

Entrepreneurs emphasize the importance of empowerment in issue resolution. Staff members are given the authority and tools to address common issues promptly. Whether it's handling billing discrepancies, addressing service delays, or managing complaints about product quality, the goal is to ensure that customers feel heard and their concerns are addressed in a timely and satisfactory manner.

Continuous Training and Development:

Customer service excellence is not a destination; it's an ongoing journey of growth and improvement. This section underscores the importance of continuous training and development for staff members, ensuring that they stay abreast of evolving customer expectations and industry trends.

The sub-chapter begins by emphasizing the dynamic nature of the mobile coffee business. With changing customer preferences, emerging trends, and evolving industry standards, staff members need to adapt continuously. Entrepreneurs instill a culture of curiosity and a proactive approach to learning, encouraging staff members to stay curious about new coffee varieties, brewing techniques, and customer engagement strategies.

Continuous training involves regular updates on menu changes, introducing new coffee offerings, and refining communication skills. Staff members are provided with opportunities for professional development, whether through workshops, online courses, or participation in industry events. This commitment to ongoing learning not only enhances the expertise of staff members but also infuses a sense of enthusiasm and passion into their roles.

Entrepreneurs recognize that engaged and motivated staff members are more likely to deliver exceptional customer service. As such, continuous training extends beyond technical skills to encompass elements of motivation, team dynamics, and personal development. Workshops on teamwork, effective collaboration, and stress management contribute to a positive work environment that, in turn, reflects in the interactions with customers.

In the mobile coffee haven, staff members are not just employees; they are the architects of a customer's experience. This sub-chapter serves as a guide to shaping these architects into orchestrators of interpersonal excellence. From understanding the art of hospitality to honing effective communication skills, leveraging product knowledge, resolving customer issues, and embracing continuous training and development, staff members become the instrumentalists in the symphony of exceptional customer service. As customers take a sip of their meticulously crafted coffee, it's not just the flavor that lingers; it's the resonance of a positive and memorable interaction that transforms a transaction into an experience.

Developing Loyalty Programs - Nurturing Reciprocal Bonds

Loyalty programs become the threads weaving reciprocal bonds between the mobile coffee haven and its patrons. This sub-chapter delves into the art of developing loyalty programs that go beyond transactional benefits.

Understanding Customer Preferences:

In the intricate dance of loyalty programs, understanding the unique preferences of the customer base is the opening step. Loyalty programs cease to be effective if they don't resonate with the patrons they aim to serve. Entrepreneurs explore nuanced strategies for deciphering these preferences, recognizing that loyalty is not a one-size-fits-all concept.

The sub-chapter initiates with the acknowledgment that the first step towards crafting an effective loyalty program is to understand the diverse tastes, expectations, and desires of the customer base. Entrepreneurs employ tools such as surveys, feedback mechanisms, and personalized interactions to gain insights into what truly matters to their patrons.

By acknowledging the distinct preferences of their customers, mobile coffee businesses can tailor loyalty programs to align with their audience's desires. Whether it's a preference for certain coffee blends, a penchant for specific add-ons, or a desire for unique experiences, entrepreneurs gain the tools to design loyalty programs that resonate on a personal level.

Designing Incentive Structures:

Loyalty programs are akin to a strategic dance, a choreography of incentives designed to encourage repeat business. Entrepreneurs guide readers in crafting incentive structures that not only attract but also retain loyal patrons. This involves understanding the behavioral triggers that drive customer engagement.

The sub-chapter explores various incentive structures, ranging from traditional punch cards to modern digital points systems. Entrepreneurs delve into the psychology of loyalty, recognizing that incentives should not only be attractive but also aligned with customer behaviors. For example, rewarding frequent visits, larger purchases, or participation in promotional events can become key elements of the loyalty dance.

Entrepreneurs recognize that the choreography of incentives is dynamic. It involves a delicate balance between offering tangible rewards and creating a sense of anticipation for the next benefit. By understanding the rhythm of their patrons' engagement, businesses can design loyalty programs that become an enticing melody, drawing customers back for the next dance.

Exclusive Offers and Events:

The allure of loyalty extends beyond mere discounts; it encompasses the enchantment of exclusive offers and events. Entrepreneurs guide readers in weaving a tapestry of exclusivity within loyalty programs, creating an atmosphere where patrons feel valued and special.

The sub-chapter explores the inclusion of exclusive offers, providing loyal customers with access to discounts, promotions, or bundled packages that are not available to the general public. Beyond discounts, entrepreneurs delve into the realm of special events, such as VIP tastings, early access to new menu items, or curated coffee experiences.

By infusing elements of exclusivity, loyalty programs become a gateway to unique and memorable experiences. These exclusive offerings not only reward loyalty but also foster a sense of belonging among patrons. It's not just about transactions; it's about creating moments that transcend the ordinary and make patrons feel like integral members of an exclusive community.

Personalized Rewards:

Loyalty is a deeply personal connection, and entrepreneurs recognize that personalized rewards are the heartbeat of effective loyalty programs. This sub-chapter explores the art of acknowledging individual patrons and tailoring rewards to their unique preferences and contributions.

The concept of personalization begins with the recognition that every patron is distinct. Entrepreneurs guide readers in designing loyalty programs that go beyond generic rewards, acknowledging the specific behaviors, preferences, and contributions of individual customers.

Entrepreneurs delve into strategies for collecting and utilizing customer data to tailor rewards. This may involve recognizing a customer's favorite blend, remembering their special requests, or acknowledging milestones in their loyalty journey. By incorporating these personalized touches, loyalty programs become more than a transactional exchange; they become a vehicle for building genuine and lasting connections.

Monitoring and Adapting Loyalty Programs:

Loyalty programs, like a well-composed symphony, evolve over time. Entrepreneurs guide readers in the importance of not only initiating but also continuously monitoring and adapting these programs. This section explores strategies for analyzing the effectiveness of loyalty incentives and making data-driven adjustments to ensure continued customer engagement.

The sub-chapter initiates with the understanding that customer preferences, market dynamics, and industry trends are dynamic. As such, loyalty programs need to adapt to stay relevant and effective. Entrepreneurs guide readers in establishing robust mechanisms for monitoring the performance of loyalty programs.

Analyzing data becomes a key aspect of this adaptive process. Entrepreneurs explore metrics such as customer engagement, redemption rates, and feedback to gain insights into the effectiveness of loyalty incentives. By leveraging analytics tools and customer feedback mechanisms, businesses can make informed decisions about refining, expanding, or introducing new elements to their loyalty programs.

Adaptability is the hallmark of successful loyalty programs. Entrepreneurs guide readers in embracing a mindset of continuous improvement, recognizing that what works today may need adjustment tomorrow. By staying attuned to the evolving needs and preferences of their patrons, businesses can ensure that their loyalty programs remain a dynamic force in nurturing reciprocal bonds.

In the realm of loyalty programs, entrepreneurs are not just crafting incentives; they are nurturing reciprocal bonds. This sub-chapter serves as a guide to creating loyalty programs that transcend transactional benefits, acknowledging the individual preferences of patrons, designing strategic incentive structures, offering exclusive experiences, providing personalized rewards, and embracing continuous monitoring and adaptation. Loyalty, in this context, becomes more than a program; it becomes a dance between a mobile coffee haven and its patrons, a harmonious exchange that goes beyond the cup and fosters a lasting and meaningful connection.

Handling Customer Feedback and Improving Services - A Feedback Symphony

In the pursuit of excellence, customer feedback becomes a valuable score, guiding the mobile coffee haven toward continuous improvement. This sub-chapter explores the art of handling feedback and using it as a catalyst for refining services.

Creating Feedback Mechanisms:

In the grand symphony of customer service, feedback is not an imposition but an invitation. Entrepreneurs guide readers in creating effective feedback mechanisms, recognizing that the input of patrons is a valuable source of insight. This section explores diverse channels for collecting feedback, from traditional suggestion boxes to modern digital platforms.

Entrepreneurs emphasize the importance of making the feedback process seamless and accessible for patrons. Whether through post-purchase surveys, interactive apps, or direct engagement during service, creating multiple touch points for feedback ensures a diverse range of perspectives. The goal is not just to collect feedback but to invite customers into a collaborative dialogue, where their voices shape the evolving narrative of the mobile coffee haven.

Analyzing Feedback Data:

Gathering feedback is only the first note in the symphony of improvement; the real harmony comes alive through analysis. Entrepreneurs delve into strategies for effectively analyzing feedback data, recognizing that the true value lies in understanding the underlying sentiments and identifying actionable insights.

The sub-chapter explores the use of analytics tools, sentiment analysis, and qualitative evaluation methods to extract meaningful trends from the feedback data. By categorizing feedback into themes, entrepreneurs gain a holistic view of the customer experience, pinpointing areas of strength and opportunities for enhancement. Analysis becomes the lens through which entrepreneurs interpret the customer's voice and transform it into a roadmap for service refinement.

Implementing Customer-Driven Changes:

Customer feedback is not just a collection of opinions; it's a catalyst for improvement. This sub-chapter unfolds as a guide to translating feedback into actionable changes. Entrepreneurs navigate the process of identifying specific areas for improvement based on customer insights, whether in menu offerings, service speed, or overall ambiance.

Entrepreneurs recognize that implementing changes requires a strategic approach. By prioritizing feedback based on its impact and feasibility, businesses can focus on the most impactful improvements first. The sub-chapter explores the importance of creating an iterative process, where continuous feedback informs an ongoing cycle of refinement.

Responsive Communication:

Acknowledging feedback is as important as implementing changes. Entrepreneurs delve into the art of responsive communication, recognizing that the way feedback is acknowledged and addressed contributes to the overall customer experience. This section provides guidance on crafting thoughtful and appreciative responses to customer feedback.

The sub-chapter emphasizes the importance of acknowledging both positive and constructive feedback. Entrepreneurs guide staff in responding promptly, expressing gratitude for positive comments, and demonstrating a commitment to addressing concerns. Responsive communication transforms feedback from a one-sided expression into a meaningful dialogue, fostering a sense of partnership between the mobile coffee haven and its patrons.

Cultivating a Culture of Continuous Improvement:

Customer feedback is not a one-time event but a continuous conversation. This section unfolds as a guide to cultivating a culture of continuous improvement within the mobile coffee business. Entrepreneurs recognize that improvement is not a destination but an ongoing journey.

The sub-chapter explores the importance of fostering a mindset where every piece of feedback, whether big or small, contributes to the evolution of services. Entrepreneurs guide readers in creating an environment where staff actively seek feedback, view it as an opportunity for growth, and embrace the challenge of constant refinement.

Entrepreneurs also explore strategies for incorporating feedback mechanisms into staff training programs, ensuring that the entire team is aligned with the ethos of continuous improvement. By cultivating a culture where feedback is embraced as a gift rather than a critique, businesses create an environment where every note in the symphony of improvement contributes to the creation of an exceptional customer experience.

In the intricate dance of customer feedback and service improvement, entrepreneurs orchestrate a symphony of continuous improvement. This sub-chapter serves as a guide to creating effective feedback mechanisms, analyzing data for actionable insights, implementing customer-driven changes, communicating responsively, and cultivating a culture where improvement is not an end goal but an ongoing journey. In this symphony, every note of customer feedback becomes a valuable contribution, guiding the mobile coffee haven toward a crescendo of excellence.

Chapter 8

Scaling and Adapting for Growth

In the journey of a mobile coffee business, the quest for growth is a dynamic and exciting phase. This chapter unfolds as a guide to scaling operations and adapting strategies for sustained expansion.

Monitoring Business Performance Metrics: Unveiling the Metrics Symphony

In the dynamic world of business, growth is not merely a goal but a continuous journey orchestrated by the harmonious blend of data-driven insights. This sub-chapter, *"Unveiling the Metrics Symphony,"* explores the art of monitoring key business performance metrics – the musical notes that guide entrepreneurs in orchestrating their mobile coffee haven's success.

Defining Key Performance Indicators (KPIs): Just as a musical composition is comprised of distinctive notes, a business's performance is defined by Key Performance Indicators (KPIs). Entrepreneurs embark on this journey by understanding and identifying critical KPIs that resonate with the rhythm of their specific business. Metrics such as revenue, customer acquisition cost, customer retention rate, and operational efficiency become the fundamental notes in the symphony of success.

Revenue serves as the melody, indicating the financial health and overall success of the mobile coffee business. Understanding *customer acquisition cost* is akin to discerning the intricate harmony, ensuring that acquiring customers aligns with sustainable financial practices. The *customer retention rate* plays the role of a recurring refrain, signifying customer loyalty and the potential for recurring revenue. Lastly, *operational efficiency* functions as the rhythm, setting the pace and ensuring smooth operations in the bustling mobile coffee haven.

Implementing Tracking Systems: With the notes identified, entrepreneurs' transition to the practical act of implementing tracking systems. Technology and analytics tools become the instruments that collect and translate these notes into actionable insights. The sub-chapter guides entrepreneurs through the selection and deployment of tracking tools, ensuring that they resonate with the unique needs and scale of the mobile coffee business.

The focus is on creating a symphony of data that is not only comprehensive but also accessible in real-time. Entrepreneurs delve into the utilization of cutting-edge technology to streamline data collection and analysis, ensuring that the pulse of the business is continuously monitored. This implementation of tracking systems transforms the business metrics into a live performance, allowing entrepreneurs to make informed decisions in the ever-changing business landscape.

Interpreting and Acting on Data: The gathering of data sets the stage, but the true symphony emerges through the interpretation and action taken based on insights. Entrepreneurs become conductors, deciphering the nuances of performance data to identify patterns, trends, and potential areas for improvement. This sub-chapter provides a guide on how to read the musical notes of metrics, translating them into actionable strategies.

Agility becomes a key theme as entrepreneurs learn to adapt strategies in response to evolving metrics. For instance, a dip in customer retention may prompt a refined customer engagement strategy. Similarly, a surge in customer acquisition cost may lead to creative marketing approaches. The dynamic feedback loop created by interpreting and acting on data ensures that the business remains in tune with the ever-changing market dynamics.

Creating a Performance Culture: In the crescendo of business growth, the importance of every team member is accentuated. Entrepreneurs are guided in fostering a performance culture within the mobile coffee business. This involves instilling an understanding of the significance of KPIs among team members, fostering a sense of ownership, and aligning individual efforts with overarching business goals.

The sub-chapter emphasizes the role of leadership in cultivating a culture where every team member contributes to the symphony of success. Entrepreneurs learn to communicate the importance of KPIs, making them an integral part of the team's daily operations. As a result, each member becomes a skilled instrumentalist, contributing to the collective performance and success of the mobile coffee haven.

"*Unveiling the Metrics Symphony*" is not just a sub-chapter; it's a guide for entrepreneurs to conduct their business operations with precision, guided by the harmonious blend of KPIs. By defining, implementing, interpreting, and fostering a performance culture, entrepreneurs transform their mobile coffee business into a symphony of success, where every note resonates with growth and prosperity.

Expanding the Menu and Services: Crafting a Culinary Symphony

In the unfolding saga of a mobile coffee business's growth, the art of expanding the menu and services is akin to crafting a culinary symphony. This sub-chapter navigates the nuances of this strategic maneuver, where entrepreneurs, as culinary conductors, orchestrate new offerings to captivate evolving audiences and enhance the mobile coffee experience.

Understanding Customer Preferences: Before introducing new melodies to the menu, entrepreneurs embark on a journey to understand the intricate notes of customer preferences. This section serves as a guide, illustrating how entrepreneurs can leverage customer feedback, analyze purchasing patterns, and conduct market research. The goal is to identify potential gaps and opportunities in the existing menu, ensuring that expansions resonate harmoniously with the desires of the customer base.

Innovative Menu Expansion: Entrepreneurs delve into the world of innovation, exploring ways to expand the menu creatively. From introducing new coffee blends and specialty beverages to incorporating complementary food items, this sub-chapter unveils the art of balancing novelty with the core identity of the mobile coffee haven. The emphasis is on crafting an expanded menu that not only delights but also remains true to the brand's essence.

Creating Signature Offerings: In the grand symphony of menu expansion, the creation of signature offerings takes center stage. Entrepreneurs learn the art of crafting unique and memorable items that become the heartbeat of the mobile coffee brand. Whether it's a signature drink infused with local flavors, a seasonal special that captures the essence of the moment, or a collaboration with local artisans, these offerings contribute to the brand's distinct identity and leave an indelible mark on the customer's experience.

Ensuring Operational Feasibility: Expansion is not solely about creativity; it's about operational feasibility. Entrepreneurs navigate the practical aspects of ensuring that the expanded menu seamlessly aligns with the capabilities of the mobile coffee truck. This involves a meticulous consideration of equipment requirements, supply chain management, and staff training. The sub-chapter provides insights into how entrepreneurs can integrate new offerings into daily operations, ensuring a smooth and efficient execution that enhances the overall customer experience.

Crafting a culinary symphony through menu expansion is not merely about adding new items; it's about creating an immersive and delightful experience for patrons. This sub-chapter serves as a guide, helping entrepreneurs navigate the complexities of understanding customer preferences, innovating with a balanced approach, creating signature offerings, and ensuring operational feasibility. By infusing creativity into the expansion process, entrepreneurs transform their mobile coffee business into a harmonious blend of flavors that resonates with both loyal and new customers alike.

Exploring New Locations and Events for Maximum Exposure: The Geographical Overture

In the grand performance of business growth, the exploration of new locations and participation in events is akin to a geographical overture, expanding the reach and resonance of the mobile coffee symphony. This sub-chapter unfolds as a comprehensive guide, revealing the art of strategic location exploration and event participation for maximum exposure and sustained success.

Conducting Location Feasibility Studies: Entrepreneurs embark on a journey of location feasibility studies, orchestrating a systematic evaluation of potential areas for expansion. This section guides entrepreneurs in defining criteria such as foot traffic, demographics, competitor presence, and local regulations. Emphasis is placed on aligning new locations with the target audience and the unique brand positioning of the mobile coffee haven. Through comprehensive feasibility studies, entrepreneurs lay the groundwork for harmonious integration into diverse geographical landscapes.

Strategic Event Participation: Events serve as dynamic stages for the mobile coffee business to showcase its performance. Entrepreneurs explore the nuances of strategic event participation, from local festivals and markets to corporate gatherings and community functions. The sub-chapter provides insights into selecting events that align seamlessly with the brand ethos, target audience, and overarching growth objectives. Through strategic event engagement, entrepreneurs create memorable experiences that resonate with diverse communities.

Utilizing Collaborations and Partnerships: Collaborations and partnerships emerge as key instruments in the geographical overture. Entrepreneurs delve into the art of fostering collaborations with local businesses, organizers, and community influencers. The section explores ways to create mutually beneficial partnerships that amplify brand visibility and enhance the mobile coffee presence in new locations. Collaborations become a strategic crescendo, enriching the symphony of the business's geographical reach.

Adapting to Seasonal and Trend-Based Opportunities: In the ever-evolving symphony of geographical exploration, entrepreneurs learn the art of adaptation to seasonal and trend-based opportunities. This sub-chapter provides practical strategies for identifying seasonal nuances and aligning offerings with emerging trends. Whether it's crafting refreshing beverages for summer events or embracing the latest coffee trends, businesses learn to orchestrate their offerings in harmony with the dynamic and trend-sensitive market.

Monitoring and Adapting Location Strategies: The symphony of growth demands a keen ear for feedback and adaptability. Entrepreneurs explore strategies for monitoring the success of new locations and event participation. Gathering customer feedback becomes a key element in refining location strategies. The sub-chapter emphasizes the importance of agility in responding to the evolving dynamics of different locations, ensuring a harmonious integration into diverse communities.

Exploring new locations and events is not just a geographical expansion; it's a symphony of strategic decisions and adaptability. This sub-chapter serves as a comprehensive guide, providing entrepreneurs with the insights and strategies needed to orchestrate a geographical overture that expands the reach of the mobile coffee symphony and resonates with diverse audiences. Through careful planning, collaboration, and adaptability, entrepreneurs set the stage for sustained growth and maximum exposure in the ever-expanding landscape of the mobile coffee business.

WISHING YOU A PROFITABLE BUSINESS AS YOU START YOUR COFFEE TRUCK BUSINESS!!!

www.ingramcontent.com/pod-product-compliance
Lightning Source LLC
Chambersburg PA
CBHW082111220526
45472CB00009B/2137